THE CHURCH OF
SAINT MARY'S, BURGH HEATH

THE FIRST 100 YEARS

ACKNOWLEDGEMENTS

This book has been made possible from the following sources and people:

St. Mary's fund raising leaflets - *Reverend Duncan Woodroffe*

St. Mary's Minutes written by *E.M. Johnson - Surrey History Centre.*

Proposed drawings of the church by J.A. Thomas - *Surrey History Centre*

Invitation to the laying of the Foundation stone - *Surrey History Centre.*

Reminiscences by *Reverend Harold Godefroy* of St. Mary's *(Burgh Heath Parish Magazines October to December 1949).*

A History of the Manor and Parish of Burgh - *S. Totman*

The collection of St. Mary's Burgh Heath Parish Magazines - Leslie and Elsie Dansey

Members of St. Mary's including Reverend Stephen Wilcockson, Reverend Sandra Faccini, Jack and Sheila Plimmer, Ralph and Mary White, David and Christine Hodges, Roger and Christine Symes for their help with proof reading and many others whose help and encouragement have made this book possible.

Members of the Banstead History Research Group including Elsie Dansey whose initial draft and valuable collection of parish magazines made this book possible, Audrey Carty for discovering a fine stained glass window, the late Ted Purver for his account of the parish magazines, Edna Touzel, Mark Cory, John Sweetman and Ted Bond.

Compiled by Ralph Maciejewski.

A catalogue record for this book is available from the British Library

ISBN 978-0-9550768

Front cover: Saint Mary from the stained glass window in St. Monica's Chapel, 2008.

Inside front cover: The interior looking east towards the Chancel, 2008.

Inside back cover: The Vicars and Curates of St. Mary's (1905 to 2008) and Timeline.

Back cover: The church from the South West, 2007.

Printed through SS Media, 88 Sandy Lane South, Wallington, Surrey SM6 9RQ

Tel: 020 8404 3922   email: info@ss-media.co.uk

CONTENTS

A MESSAGE FROM THE VICAR OF THE PARISH

Dear Friends,

Thank you for buying a copy of our St. Mary's Centenary book!

It gives me great pleasure to commend it as a record of 100 years of Christian worship in the Burgh Heath Community. My own part in the story is a very small one, only going back a few years, since the Parish of Howell Hill offered to help the local community keep its local church going and growing.

I am privileged to be the Vicar of the Parish as St. Mary's reaches this important milestone in its life. The church came perilously close to not reaching this birthday! It was down for closure in 2001, but – with God's enabling, and in partnership with St. Mark's Tattenham Corner (in whose parish Burgh Heath previously lay) – we have been able to give St. Mary's a new lease of life which bodes well for the next hundred years.

The invention of the motor car, and its availability to virtually every family, has enhanced all of our lives. However, there is a cost. The track that once meandered through the village of Burgh Heath has been transformed into the virtual motorway that the A217 is now. It has carved up the old community, and "marooned" the village and its church to the east of the road. It was almost the death-knell of St. Mary's – but we survived!

Today, we find ourselves occupying a very prominent site on the main road, and still offering a service to parishioners on both sides of it and further afield. Like all the local residents, we are learning to live with the challenge of a major trunk road carrying a huge volume of high speed traffic.

In this book, you will trace the story of how a quiet village and its church came to find itself in this exposed position, and yet has not only survived, but has determinedly maintained its community life through all the changes of time. At St. Mary's, we look forward to being part of the community and working for the welfare of all local people for many more years to come.

This book will be an inspiration to all of us as we face this challenge together. Enjoy the read!

Your sincere friend and Vicar,

Steve Wilcockson

Vicar, St. Paul's Howell Hill with St. Mary's Burgh Heath.

CHAPTER 1
THE EARLY HISTORY OF BURGH HEATH

In the area which is now known as the village of Burgh Heath, in the neighbourhood of the ancient common which bears that name, there would have been little more in the Middle Ages than a few farms and cottages. The road from London towards Reigate Hill would have been rough depending for its repair on the inhabitants of the parish of Banstead.

The area had very early associations with the Monastery of Chertsey, to which a grant was made on its foundation in AD 727 of land *"apud Benesteda cum Suthmersfelde"*. This was confirmed by King Edgar in AD 967. The field name *"Suthmersfelde"* would survive for centuries in slightly varied forms, though the grant itself evidently lapsed, possibly as the result of the reallocation of properties following the Norman conquest.

THE FIRST CHURCH

The monastic connection was renewed during the reign of Henry I (1100 - 1135), when the Lord of the Manor of Banstead, Tirel de Maniers, granted the Advowson of Banstead to the Priory of Saint Mary Overie at Southwark, a House of Augustinian Canons whose church is now Southwark cathedral. With the advowson, the priory acquired the land formerly granted to Chertsey Abbey, now known as *Summerfield* or *Southmerfield* and they built there a rectory at or near the present Canons Farm in Canons Lane. They were also given the Manor of North Tadworth, a sub-manor of Banstead. A later Lord of the Manor of Banstead, Nigel de Mowbray, confirmed this grant and also granted to them *"the church of Burgh"*. This was a building near what is now the junction of Tattenham Way and Reigate Road. The Priory continued to *"present"* clergy to this small church until 1414, although as early as 1379 it was reported to be in a ruinous condition.

THE CHAPEL OF ST. LEONARD

Another church in the vicinity was one dedicated to Saint Leonard and attached to another sub-manor, that of Preston. It stood where Chapel Grove now is, off Merland Rise near Tattenham Corner. Like the church of Burgh, this seems to have fallen into disuse and ultimately to have been demolished leaving this area without any church accessible to the public.

Opposite
The chapel at Nork House in 1812.

The parishoners of Burgh Heath were allowed to worship in the chapel by Mrs. Helen Colman of Nork Park from 1905 as the school room in the Burgh Heath School proved unsatisfactory for conducting church services..

Above
Nork House by Prosser, in about 1811.

The house was built in 1715 by Christopher Buckle and over the years it became the residence of Lord and Lady Arden, the Earl of Egmont and from 1890, Frederick Colman of the mustard family.

EVENTS IN THE 16TH TO 18TH CENTURIES

In 1539 the Priory of Saint Mary Overie was dissolved. It seems that the priory had for some considerable time ceased to have any direct connection with the rectory and land at Burgh Heath. These had been leased to members of the Richbell family for at least forty years. In 1524, the rectory building, the farmland and the rights to tithes had been leased to Richard Moys and his wife Elizabeth. The Advowson of Banstead however, remained attached to the Canons in right of their ownership of the property.

After the Priory of Saint Mary Overie was dissolved, Moys bought the property from the Crown along with the advowson, which from that time passed to successive owners of the property. At some time the rectory building ceased to exist.

By 1615 the property and the advowson had become vested in the Buckle family and became a part of the large estate held by them along with their mansion of Great Burgh, which stood on or near the present Home Farm Close. They continued to own the land and the advowson until 1845. They also acquired land at Nork and in 1740 erected a mansion known as Nork House which became their main residence.

PROVISION FOR WORSHIP IN THE 19TH CENTURY

In 1812 the Nork Estate was bought by Lord Arden who had held it as lessee since 1784. The Great Burgh estate was also leased and in 1819 Lord Arden acquired that lease so that he was in possession of the combined Nork and Great Burgh estates. In 1847 his successor, who had inherited the title of Earl of Egmont as well as the Nork estate, bought the Great Burgh estate, and with it, the advowson of Banstead.

In the meantime, the Dowager Lady Arden had enabled a Church of England school to be opened in 1857 on common land west of the Sutton to Reigate Road, having donated the site and provided the school with an endowment of £6 per annum. The school was occasionally used as a place of worship and from 1865 Sunday evening services were held there.

In 1884 the wife of the Reverend E.V. Buckle, one of a succession of members of the Buckle family to hold the post of Vicar of Banstead, provided a new school, St. Mary's Church School at Burgh Heath. This was larger than the original school and was intended to serve the dual purposes of a weekday school and Sunday worship. One end of the schoolroom had a temporary altar and choir stall.

Below
St. Mary's Church School at Burgh Heath provided by wife of the Reverend E.V. Buckle in 1884. It is now divided into a number of apartments and called Chips Folly.

SERVICES IN ST. MARY'S CHURCH SCHOOL

Harold Godefroy was the assistant Curate of Banstead and in charge of the district comprising Burgh Heath, Nork Park and the part of Banstead in the Garratts Hall region from 1905 to 1917. In his reminiscences, published in the October 1949 edition of the parish magazine, he recalled that in 1905:

> *"..our services were held in the Burgh Heath School Room, but no-one felt that it had quite the same atmosphere as a Church. It is true we had some choir-stalls and a very small choir, which was practically a one-man choir and this one man had a harsh overpowering voice with which nobody could possibly compete. Unfortunately, he was the most regular attendant, for though he lifted up his voice to the utmost, it quite failed to lift up the hearts of the few who tried to worship with us. Mr. W. Martin, of Kethlen, acted as organist and I always admired his endurance."*

In 1890 the Nork and Great Burgh estates were bought by Mr. F. E. Colman. As St. Mary's School in Burgh Heath proved unsatisfactory for church purposes the Colman family increasingly allowed services to be held in their private chapel in Nork House.

Towards the end of the 19th century the parish church of All Saints, Banstead was frequently overcrowded due to the gradual increase in the local population. A number of plans to enlarge the old church were proposed but none of them was regarded as anything but unsatisfactory as they would have destroyed its unique and picturesque character. It was even suggested that the best plan would be to pull down the old church and erect in its place a much larger and more modern building. None of the inhabitants of Banstead would have considered, far less sanctioned, such an act of vandalism. The only viable alternative was to build a second church elsewhere in the parish.

In 1901, Mr. Frederick Lambert of Garratts Hall and Mr. Charles H. Garton of Banstead Wood, each purchased a plot of land on the east side of the Brighton Road in Burgh Heath. The two plots, which were contiguous, formed a convenient site for a permanent church. This was the first definite step taken towards the building of a church at Burgh Heath.

Unfortunately at the time, the Vicar of All Saints, the Reverend E.V. Buckle, due to his advanced age and increasing infirmity, was unable to undertake the task of getting a new church built. Also, in 1902, Mr. Frederick Lambert died without making any legal provision for the allocation of his plot of land which he had purchased for the purposes of a church.

The Reverend E.V. Buckle died in 1905 and was succeeded in the same year by the Reverend Duncan Woodroffe.

THE FIRST STEPS

On Ascension Day 24 May 1906, the Reverend Duncan Woodroffe, organised a public meeting in Banstead in connection with the gift of a Church Institute to the village of Banstead. It was at that meeting that a resolution was brought forward and unanimously passed in favour of making the preliminary steps towards the erection of a suitable church at Burgh Heath. A committee was then appointed for the purpose which consisted of the Clergy: Revd. Duncan Woodroffe, Vicar of All Saints Banstead, Harold Godefroy, Assistant Curate; Churchwardens: Mr. Stephen Wingrove, Mr. Henry Knibbs, and subsequently in 1908, Mr. T. G. Orton;

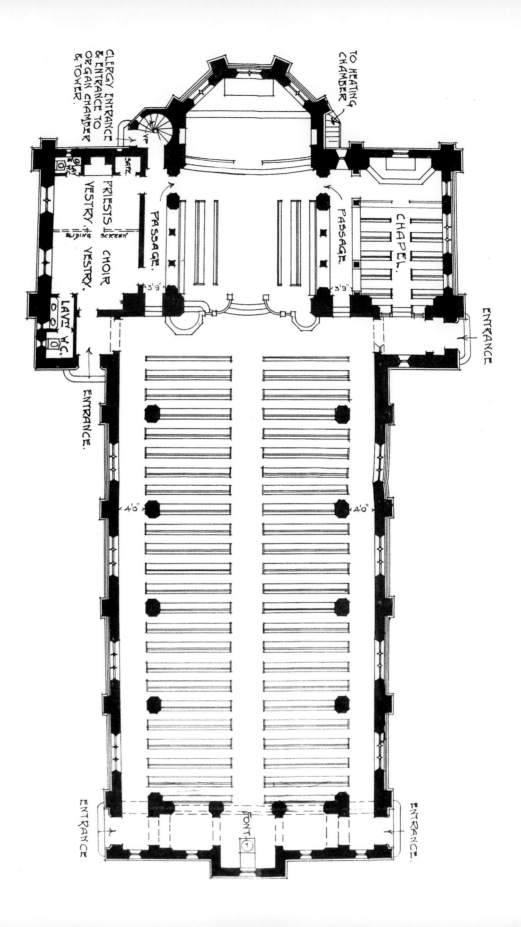

CLERGY ENTRANCE
& ENTRANCE TO
ORGAN CHAMBER
& TOWER.

TO HEATING
CHAMBER

SAFE.

VESTRY.

PRIESTS
VESTRY.

CHOIR
VESTRY.

SLIDING SCREEN.

PASSAGE.

PASSAGE.

CHAPEL.

3'9"

3'9"

LAVY.
W.C.

ENTRANCE.

ENTRANCE.

4'0"

4'0"

ENTRANCE.

ENTRANCE.

FONT.

and representative parishioners: Messrs. C. H. Blake, Gordon Colman, Charles H. Garton, E. M. Johnson, P. G. Russell, William Martin, Maynard Taylor and Howard W. Trollope.

The new committee also agreed to build the church on the site originally selected. Mr. Garton presented his plot of land with the other half of the site being subsequently acquired by purchase from the Executors of the late Mr. F. Lambert.

At the first meeting of the committee, suggestions were put forward to build either a temporary structure or just a small church which could be subsequently enlarged as the population increased. Mrs. Helen Colman of Nork Park insisted however, that a worthy church and one big enough to meet the future needs of the district should be built. The committee hence agreed unanimously to build a good and complete church at once that would be of a substantial permanent character and of sufficient size to meet the requirements of an increasing population.

RAISING FUNDS

A church building fund was then immediately set up and a generous contribution of £2000 was donated by Mrs. Helen Colman of Nork Park and her two sons, Mr. Gordon Colman and Mr. Nigel Colman, on the condition

that a complete church should be built at a total cost of not less than £5000. Other additional amounts were also promised so that by July 1906 nearly £4000 had been raised.

The church was built from the designs by Mr. J. Alick Thomas, architect, with the contractors being Messrs Roberts of Islington. The estimated cost of the building, including internal fitments but excluding the tower was £5000.

At a public meeting in Banstead on 15th December 1906, the Bishop of Winchester presided at a public meeting for the express purpose of furthering the scheme of the building of the church. He entirely approved and warmly advocated the proposal and expressed his hope that it would meet with the support of all the parishioners and that he would very shortly be called to lay the foundation stone.

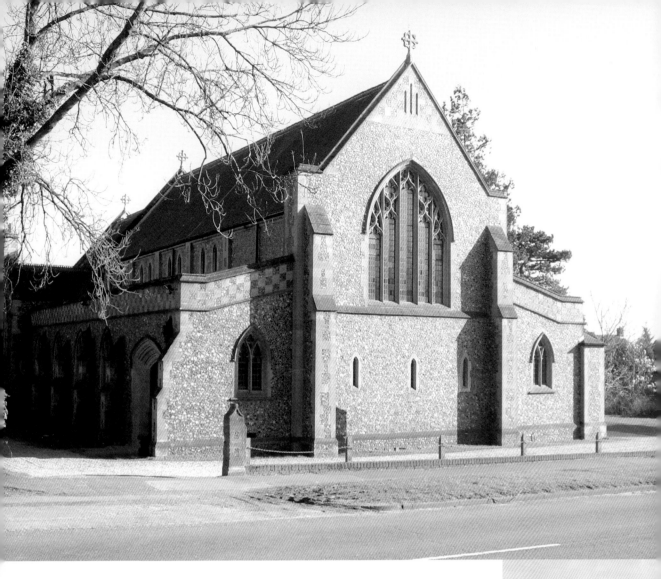

An account was opened at the Banstead branch of the London and Provincial Bank in the joint names of the Rev. Duncan Woodroffe, F. Gordon Colman and Charles H. Garton as treasurers. Promises of contributions or cheques were to be forwarded to them or to any member of the committee. The donations could be paid by instalments or spread over two years if more convenient.

Nearly everybody in the Parish and throughout the district had a hand in building the church. Many, including children, contributed generously to the building fund according to their means and the gifts of the poorest entailed real sacrifice. The subscription list of 1907 on pages 16 to 17 in this book lists those who contributed pence as well as hundreds of pounds.

In addition to the direct subscriptions, various efforts were made at different times to raise the necessary funds. One of the most important was

Above
The west end of the church as it appears today. The south porch has substantial walls which allows for a tower to be built at a later date.

9

Right
The formal invitation to the laying of the foundation stone.

*By courtesy of
Surrey History Centre*

a grand fete organised at Nork Park on St. Swithin's Day, July 15th, 1908. On the day there were ominous clouds at the opening which caused the Duchess of Albany, who opened the fête, to comment that she hoped it was not going to be a water fête! Fortunately it was not, and as people came from far and wide it proved to be a great success.

BLESSING OF THE SITE

On Sunday afternoon, March 8 1908, a short service was held on the building plot as a Benediction of the Site at which prayers were offered for a blessing on the work. The building of the church was then started the next day and continued without interruption until it was complete.

LAYING OF THE FOUNDATION STONE

Seven weeks after building commenced, the foundation stone for the church was laid. On Monday April 27 1908, the ceremony of the laying of the Foundation Stone was performed by Mrs. Colman with the Reverend Archer George Hunter, Canon of Winchester, Rural Dean of Leatherhead and Vicar of Christ Church Epsom, conducting the religious service supported by the clergy of the parish and immediate neighbourhood in the presence of a large gathering of parishioners.

THE CHURCH BUILDING

The church was built in a restrained gothic style in stone and knapped flint without a tower or spire. The flints came by rail to Kingswood station with the men on the building site being paid 4d per hour (about 1.6 pence in present day money) to do the knapping, that is splitting the whole flint with a hammer so that the veined glass-like surface is obtained when incorporated in the wall.

The exterior buttresses of the church which give it such a neat appearance were not just put there for appearance sake. The site was partially waterlogged and the buttresses were therefore an essential part of the structure. Due to the nature of the subsoil the building is supported below ground on arches.

The west wall has a large window but no entrance door, the entrance to the church being through the two doors at the west end of each of the north and south walls. The interior is plain neo-gothic with a wooden barrel-vault roof. Interior lighting is aided by clerestory windows.

CONVEYANCE OF THE CHURCH SITE

The church and site were conveyed by the then Trustees, Reverend Duncan Woodroffe, Mr. Gordon Colman and Mr. E. M. Johnson to the Ecclesiastical Commissioners by a deed executed on 2 December 1908. By the end of 1908 the church was built.

THE DEDICATION AND CONSECRATION OF THE CHURCH

On Sunday January 17 1909, the last service was held in the private chapel in Nork Park after which the consecration was transferred to St. Mary's. The chapel was then closed. In lieu of the Nork Park chapel, the south chancel aisle of the church was reserved for the accommodation of Mrs. Helen Colman and her family, household and dependants. In the petition for this Consecration of the Church it is stated that:

> "The new Church affords accommodation to the extent of 350 sittings, 326 to remain free and unappropriated, the remainder being those in the South Chancel Aisle, which is proposed to be appropriate by faculty to be issued from the Consistorial Court for the separate use of Helen Colman of Nork Park in the said Parish of Banstead (widow of the late

Left
The foundation stone bearing the inscription:
Ad Majorem Gloriam Dei.
MDCCCCVIII

To the Greater Glory of God. 1908

The foundation stone was laid on Monday April 27 1908 by Mrs. Helen Colman of Nork Park with the Reverend Archer George Hunter, Canon of Winchester, conducting the religious service.

Frederick Edward Colman Esquire) and her lawful descendants as long as she or they be residents within the present limits of the Parish of Banstead."

On Saturday afternoon, January 23 1909, Doctor Hubert Ryle, Bishop of Winchester, performed the solemn official and religious ceremony of Dedication, and licensed the Church for the administration of the Sacraments. The united choirs of All Saints and of St. Mary's took part in the service. Twenty neighbouring clergy from the Diocese of Winchester and from the adjacent Diocese of Southwark joined in the Bishops Procession. The church was packed by the large congregation present.

In the course of his sermon the Bishop observed that they were more fortunate than most parishes, as they had built a church which was larger than the needs of the moment. It was a rule of the Church, though not an absolute one, not to consecrate a building so long as there was a debt on it, hence, as there was a sum of £600 still to provide, the service that afternoon was one of dedication and not consecration. He had no doubt, however, that those who by their self-denial and self-sacrifice had enabled that church to be completed in so comparatively short a time would not rest until the debt had been paid, and then the building could be consecrated. On the following Sunday, the Holy Communion was celebrated and St. Mary's became the centre of the religious worship of the district.

The church was finally consecrated in a ceremony performed by Edward Stuart Talbot, Bishop of Winchester on 16th December, 1911.

Opposite
The south chancel in 2008. It was reserved for Mrs. Helen Colman her family, household and dependants until she left the area.

Mrs. Colman sold the Nork Estate in 1923 and moved out of the area. The south chancel was then converted to a chapel dedicated to St. Monica in 1928 due to the generosity of Miss Florence Bervon, Headmistress of St. Monica's school, who was a devoted supporter and sometime Churchwarden of the Church.

Left
The service led by Reverend Sandra Faccini on Sunday April 27 2008 to celebrate the centenary of the laying of the foundation stone.

13

CHAPTER 3

GIFTS TO THE CHURCH

One of the most striking things about the building of St. Mary's church was the cooperation between the large land owning families in the area, the various dignitaries, and most of all, the ordinary folk of Banstead and Burgh Heath. It was after all, the first new church in the Parish for many centuries and so everyone gave generously according to their means with the gifts of the poorest entailing real sacrifice.

The list of subscriptions to the church fund, shown overleaf, makes fascinating reading. In particular, the small donations of 3d, 6d, and 1 shilling donated by those who for whom such amounts made a difference between eating or going without. Most of the inhabitants of Burgh Heath were principally employed as agricultural workers on the large estates of Nork Park and Banstead Woods and as a consequence their earnings were low.

In addition to donations of money, a number of gifts were donated to the church by various members of the parish. These ranged from substantial items such as a font, an altar, marble for the sanctuary, chairs, kneelers and silverware to essential small items such as alms dishes, alms bags, tables, vases and a book for recording the minutes of church proceedings..

THE FONT

This was a gift to the new church from funds raised by the children of the parish. There is no record as to how much was raised but it must have been a substantial sum judging by the size of the font. It is placed at the west end of the church midway between the north and south doors.

According to the Vestry minutes, when the Bishop of Guildford, Golding Bird, visited the Church in 1933, he noticed that the font was not covered and instructed that a cover be placed over it. Major Scott-Barrett and Mr. Tree were tasked with the matter which was resolved by Mr. Rogers offering to supply a cover at a cost of £2.10s.

The first baptisms recorded in the new church began on 24 January 1909, when Henrietta and Robert Wessom, a stud groom from Banstead, took their son, Ernest George, to the Christening. They were followed by Mary Ann and William James Blunden, from 16 Oatlands Road, who had their daughter christened Mary Ann Phyllis.

Opposite
The font which was a gift to the Church from the children of the Parish.

The lid of the font was added in 1933. It was supplied by Mr. Rogers at a cost of £2.10s.

SUBSCRIPTION LIST.

	£	s.	d.
Mrs. Colman)			
Mr. F. G. Colman }	2000	0	0
Mr. N. C. D. Colman)			
Mr. Garton	525	0	0
Mr. Wingrove	105	0	0
Mr. Johnson	105	0	0
Sir Ralph Neville	105	0	0
Mr. Martin	50	0	0
The Vicar	50	0	0
Mr. Robertson-Rodger	50	0	0
Mr. Knibbs	25	0	0
Mr. C. H. Beall	20	0	0
Mr. P. G. Russell	20	0	0
Mr. Maynard Taylor	25	0	0
Mr. Maynard Taylor and Family (specific)	100	0	0
Captain Acland	25	0	0
Mr. Adams	10	10	0
Mr. Alston	5	5	0
Hon. Mrs. Arthur	30	0	0
Mrs. Benyon	25	0	0
Mr. Clay	10	10	0
Mr. Coe	10	0	0
Miss Garton (tableaux)	37	0	0
Rev. Harold Godefroy	2	2	0
Mr. Walter Gibbons...	50	0	0
Miss Griswold	100	0	0
Mr. Glass	10	10	0
Mr. Hills	1	0	0
Mr. Leaning	21	0	0
Mr. Lailey	10	0	0
Mr. Lightbody	10	10	0
Mr. Henry Lambert	50	0	0
Mrs. Maitland (School Chapel Offertory)	4	8	1
Miss Mason...	25	0	0
Miss Mason's Pupils, past and present...	21	0	0
Mr. Pringle	10	0	0
Mrs. Purvis	5	0	0
Mr. Herbert Reid	50	0	0
Mr. A. L. Russell	10	0	0
Mr. Trollope	25	0	0
Mrs. Venn	0	5	0
Cards per Burgh Heath Local Committee	31	11	8
Cards per Rose Hill School	3	13	0
Burgh Heath Church School Entertainment	15	0	0
	£3789	4	9

Cards per Burgh Heath Local Committee.

COLLECTED BY MR. T. MARTIN.—W. Anchor 2s. 6d., H. Sandalls 1s. 6d., C. L. H. Shallcrass 5s., S. Sawkins 6d., N. Anscombe 6d., Mrs. A. 6d., J. Phillips 1s., K.L. 6d., A.L. 2s. 6d., H. J. Russell 6d., Miss Barber 6d., A. Law 1s., Mr. Reed 1s., Mrs. Reed 1s., M. Gurney 2d., W. Sallis 6d., Mrs. Wellman 6d., Baker 2d., Hunter 2d., Mr. Barber 1s., Mrs. Barber 6d., Mrs. Langridge 6d., E. Skelton 1s., Mr. Whitak 6d., Mrs. Freeman 1s., Miss Head 1s., W. T. Adams 1s., E.S. 1s., Mr. Coppock 1s., Mr. Turner 6d., Mrs. J. Blunden 6d., Mr. Martin 1s., Mrs. Martin 1s., M. P. and F. Martin 6d., H. Reed 3d., Mr. Reed 6d., Mrs. Reed 6d., R. Reed 6d., F. Knight 6d., Mr. Hunter 2d., Miss A. Wheeler 1s., Miss E. Hale 5s., Miss D. Langridge 6d., Miss E. Langridge 6d., Mrs. Tilling 1s., Mrs. Bassom 6d., total £2 2s. 11d.

Right and opposite
The list of the donations collected for the church fund.

By courtesy of Surrey History Centre

COLLECTED BY MR. J. WOOD.—L. A. Wood 1s., H. Wood 6d., C.H. 6d., A. Blaber 6d., H. Avis 6d., H. Culver 6d., J. Wood 1s., R. Wood 1s., Mrs. Hamlin 2s. 6d., Mrs. Chandler 2s. 6d., total 10s. 6d.

COLLECTED BY MR. F. WOOD.—Mr. and Mrs. F. Barber 2s., Mr. and Mrs. S. Blunden 1s., Mr. and Mrs. Phillips 1s., F. Foster 1s., Mr. and Mrs. W. Blunden 1s., Mrs. W. L. Tugwell 1s., Mrs. Sandalls 1s., total 8s.

COLLECTED BY MR. TITTERINGTON.—J. Titterington 5s., Mrs. Titterington 5s., A Friend 2s., E. Penfold 5s., Jesse Hillman 1s., Mrs. Blaker 1s., total 19s.

COLLECTED BY MR. CHANDLER.—G. Chandler 2s., E. Chandler 2s., M. Chandler 1s., total 5s.

COLLECTED BY MR. E. CULVER.—Mr. and Mrs. J. Turner 1s., Mrs. E. Culver 1s., Mr. E. Culver 1s., Frank Culver 6d., total 3s. 6d.

COLLECTED BY MR. A. CULVER.—G. Ethridge 6d., C. Hare 2s., L. Sturt 4d., M. Webb 6d., A. and E. Culver 2s. 6d., L. Cordwell 6d., total 6s. 4d.

COLLECTED BY MR. BARBER.—W. Barber 6d., E. Parker 6d., H. Parker 6d., Mrs. Wood 3d., F. Muggeridge 6d., E. Smart 3d., F. Ibbetson 6d., E. Day 2d., A. Farley 6d., Roffey 3d., R. Muggeridge 3d., Blunden 3d., total 4s. 5d.

COLLECTED BY MR. MAYS.—C. Mays 2s. 6d., E. Mays 2s. 6d., Mrs. C. Mays 2s. 6d., Miss Smith 5s., Mary Johnson 1s., Max Johnson 1s., Mrs. Johnson 5s., Mr. Johnson 5s., total £1 4s. 6d.

COLLECTED BY MR. H. PYE.—Mr. and Mrs. Hawkins 1s. 6d., Mrs. F. Hawkins 1s., Mrs. Rumsey 1s., Mr. Pye 1s., total 4s. 6d.

COLLECTED BY MR. SANDALLS.—A. Wheeler 1s., F. Privett 6d., Nellie Pointer 1s., Mrs. Harmach 6d., A Friend 6d., Fred Millington 1s., Mrs. Freeman 1s., H. S. Wapling 1s., Mrs. Liddington 6d., Mr. Campbell Smith 1s., Mrs. Morris (Fox) 1s., A. Balcomb 1s., Boniface 2s., Charlie Russell 2s., Miss Shove 6d., Miss England 6d., Miss Beadle 1s., Mrs. Runcieman 6d., Miss E. Beadle 6d., Mrs. Foster 6d., Mrs. A. Farley 6d., Miss N. Cox 6d., Mrs. Chatterton 6d., Mrs. Lambert's servant 6d., Mrs. W. Clark 6d., Miss Strudwick 6d., Miss Dancy 6d., Mrs. C. Newington £1, R.C.M. 1s., W.D.M. 1s., A.B. 1s., P.B. 1s., W.C. 3d., L.C.F. 6d., E.A. 1s., W.E. 1s., G.G.K. 2s. 6d., Mrs. Weeks 9d., Miss Eden 10s., Cardus 3d., E.C. 6d., M.M. 6d., W.M. 3d., K.P. 1s., W.P. 6d., Mr. C. 6d., W.F. 6d., Pashley 5s., English 10s., Bertie Sandalls 1s., D. M. Everett 6d., Mrs. Cracknell 6d., K. Gibson 1s., Mrs. S. Newington 1s., Mr. Darling 6d., Mr. A. Balchin, sen., 6d., Mrs. Alec Shove 1s., Mr. J. Burberry 6d., Mrs. Darling 1s., Mrs. S. Gilbert 2s., Thomas Grason 2s. 6d., Mr. Booetius 2s., Mrs. Matthews 1s., Mrs. Edgeler 1s., Mr. A. Penfold 1s., Mrs. A. Penfold 1s., Mrs. H. Palmer 1s., Mrs. Gibson 1s., Mrs. Hopson 6d., Mrs. Coppock 1s., Miss Knight (Walton) 1s., Mrs. Dench 6d., Mrs. Henry Rawles 1s., Mr. Bailey 5s., Mrs. Garner 1s., Mrs. Payne 6d., Mrs. Tipston (Kingswood) 5s., Mrs. Moberly Bell (London) 5s., Mrs. Ward (Kingswood) 2s. 6d., total £6 3s.

COLLECTED BY MR. AYLETT.—H.C. £2 2s., F. G. Colman £2 2s., N. C. Colman £2 2s., S. Colman £5, R. Wesson 10s., T. Elkington 10s., C. E. Smith 10s., L. Benson £2 2s., A. Benson £2 2s., Charles Nightingale £1, F. Aylett £1 2s., total £19.

Cards per Rose Hill School.

Williams 6s., G. Holyman 1s., Bamber 1s., Hankey 5s., Wilkinson 2s., Bower 1s. 6d., Round 2s., Jones 3s. 6d., Thorp 1s. 3d., R. King 1s., Marzetti £1, Bishop 1s. 1d., Hoyle 1s. 4d., M. C. Jones 2s. 6d., G. Hedderwick 1s. 8d., A. Hahn 2s., B. K. Smith 1s. 9d., Bickford 5s. 6d., L. Browning 3s., Marsden 2s., Harford 2s., P. K. Smith 1s. 9d., Gray 2s., Brincherhop 3d., Vosper 1s, Heaver 6d., total £3 13s.

Three weeks later, on 14 February, Agnes and Frederick Spencer Guy, a groom from Burgh Heath, had their daughter, who was born on Christmas Day, christened and appropriately named Noelle Kathleen.

On the 3rd of April 1909, Henry John Leaning, a surveyor from Copthorne, and his wife, Thomassin Edith, from Burgh Heath, had their daughter, born on 16 January, christened Daphne Thomassin.

Three baptisms followed on 11 April.

In all, over the period 1910 to 1914, the number of baptisms each year varied from a maximum of twenty-nine in 1911, to twelve in 1912. The total for 1911 was not equalled during the Great War and the total went down to twelve again in 1917. Seventeen baptisms took place in 1918 and twenty the following year.

THE ALTAR

The original altar was presented to the church by the Rector and Churchwardens of Carshalton. In June 1909 it was replaced by a gift of an oak altar with a carving of the Last Supper on the front from Mr. Maynard

Taylor and his family. The fine altar is dedicated to the daughters of D. Aldersey and Louisa Taylor and dated 1909. One side of the altar bears the following inscription:

To the Glory of God
and in loving memory of
SOPHIA LOUISA NOLAN
and
CHARLOTTE HENRIETTA TAYLOR
daughters of
D. ALDERSEY AND LOUISA TAYLOR
of the Oaks, Woodmansterne.

"I believe in the Communion of Saints"
1909

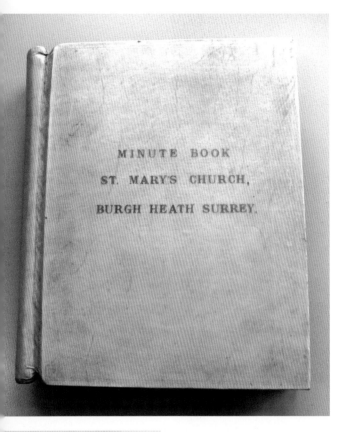

THE ORGAN

Another welcome gift was that of an organ. As the chapel in Nork House was no longer used Mrs. Colman kindly loaned the organ from the chapel to the new church. This was later replaced in 1915 by the present day organ.

SUBSTANTIAL GIFTS

A number of substantial gifts were donated to the new Church. These included the rough Sussex marble for the Sanctuary, the area containing the main altar, donated by Mr. Uvedale Lambert from his quarry at Bletchingley, 300 chairs and 300 kneelers donated by Mr. Charles Garton, the Lectern donated by Mr. S. Wingrove, Churchwarden of Banstead, a silver chalice and patten donated by Mr. W. Martin, 50 copies of Hymns Ancient and Modern, an Altar book donated by Captain Taylor and the Bible for the Lectern by Mrs. H. Colman.

Above
The Minute Book for St. Mary's Church presented to the Church on March 13 1909 by Mr. E. M. Johnson.

By courtesy of Surrey History Centre.

Opposite
The Nave with the Lectern, donated by Mrs. Colman, in the foreground.

OTHER GIFTS AND DONATIONS

Many other gifts and donations were given to the Church. These included the Minutes book, donated by Mr. E. M. Johnson, from which the early history of the Church is recorded; the Sanctuary candlesticks made by Mr. W. Martin and donated by him together with linen vestments; a reading desk donated by Mrs. Maitland (from the school chapel, Banstead Hall); the Communicants' kneeler donated by Mrs. Henry Lambert; an alms dish donated by Mrs.Wingrove; white alms bags donated by Mrs.Runel; a white burse, and silk veil and lace fair linen cloth donated by Mrs. Taylor; a green burse and silk veil donated by Mrs. Baltiscombe; corporal and purificators donated by Miss Simmons and an altar desk and vases donated by the Reverend D.Woodroffe.

The cassocks and surplices for the Church Choir were purchased from the proceeds of a fund subscribed to by parishioners and collected at a Christmas Carol party organised by Mr. Pinnock, the schoolmaster of the Church School.

CHAPTER 4

THE EARLY YEARS

By January 1909 the church had been built and on Friday evening, January 8th, a public meeting was held in the Burgh Heath School for the election of officers to the church. At the meeting, the Reverend Duncan Woodroffe, Vicar of All Saints, Banstead, proposed that the Reverend Harold Godfrey should make St. Mary's his particular care in conjunction with the Vicar. He also proposed that for the present, no official Wardens were to be appointed. Instead, a large body of sidesmen would be formed to act as an advisory and administrative Church Committee.

In addition, it was resolved that the South Chancel Aisle was to be reserved for the use of Mrs. Colman and the people of Nork in lieu of the private chapel at Nork and that all the sittings in the Nave should be free but that the Sidesmen should have the power to reserve seats, until the commencement of the Service, for the families of the regular members of the congregation.

A resolution was proposed, seconded and carried unanimously that the proposed scheme was approved by the meeting. The following Parishioners were then elected as Sidesmen to serve until Easter 1909 when they would be eligible for re-election:

> Mr. Aylett of Nork Park
> Mr. Bachelor of Oatlands Road
> Mr. C.H. Beele of Brighton Road
> Mr. Gordon Colman of Nork Park
> Mr. Nigel Colman of Nork Park
> Mr. E.M. Johnson of Wood Lodge
> Mr. W. Martin of Kethlen
> Mr. P.Q. Russell of Heathdene
> Mr. Sandells of Oatlands Road
> Captain Taylor of Can Hatch
> Mr. Tittering of Nork Farm

A THEOLOGICAL CLASH

In the October 1947 edition of the Burgh Heath Parish magazine, Harold Godefroy recollected that in the early days of the St. Mary's Church, Mr. Birch played the organ and trained the choir. However, in his opinion, in all

Opposite
St. Mary's Church in the early years viewed from the Brighton Road.

his time at St. Mary's, the choir never seemed to reach anything approaching the standard at All Saints', not even after Mrs. Colman had given a fine organ in 1915, built by Hill and Co.

He also recounted an event that:

"..left a sadness in my heart ever since, and, much as I feel inclined to gloss it over, it seems only right to state the facts quite plainly. We met with a reverse which crippled the work for years."

He continued:

"When we began at St. Mary's with a Sung Eucharist and the use of the vestments prescribed by the Prayer Book, we were led to think that the Colman family at least did not disapprove of our action. I rather think that before long some outside influence was brought to bear upon them, and it ended in an ultimatum from them, that unless we at St. Mary's fell into line with the use at the Parish Church they would feel it their duty to withdraw.

I had always had the greatest admiration for Mrs. Colman, her sound judgment and Christian spirit. But her position had made her autocratic, and, once having made up her mind, nothing that could be said by the Vicar and myself (and you may be sure we made every attempt) would lead her to change it. Here was a great shock to us and we found ourselves in a very awkward fix.

We had to choose between two evils:

(1) If we refused to give way it would means the loss to St. Mary's, not only of the Colman family and household, but of a number of others who would, I knew, feel it right to take the same attitude.

(2) If we complied it would be taken as a sign of weakness on our part and an acceptance of the idea that he who pays the piper has the right to call the tune.

After prayerful consideration, and after consultation with others whose opinions we valued, we chose the latter course. I must admit that I was not happy about it at the time, and never have been happy about it since. My great friend, Mr. Martin, took it so much to heart that he felt he could no longer act as Sacristan, though he was not the sort of man to give up his worship with us."

A NEW CHURCH ORGAN

At Easter 1915, the organ brought over from the Burgh Heath School was replaced by a fitted and much finer instrument. The instrument, made by one of the finest organ makers in the country W. Hill and Son, was fitted in the north chancel, next to the vestry. It was donated by Mrs. Helen Colman and her sons to St. Mary's Church in memory of her late husband, Frederick Colman, who died on 1 January 1900 aged 58. A brass plaque on an adjacent pillar records this fact.

At a meeting of the Church Council on 22 May 1915 a very hearty vote of thanks was passed to Mrs. Colman, Mr. Gordon Colman and Mr. Nigel Colman for their very generous gift of a new organ.

The organ, which has 2 manuals, is alleged to have been one of the finest instruments in Surrey. Today, it is the only traditional pipe organ in the district as all other churches now use electronic organs or keyboards that require little or no maintenance.

EVENTS DURING THE GREAT WAR (1914-1918)

Harold Godefroy also recounted life at the start of the Great War in 1914:

"Soon after the first Great War broke a battalion of the London Fusiliers was quartered in railway carriages at Tattenham Corner Station. On Sunday mornings the men marched across to St. Mary's, and the sound of their band brought most of the village out of doors to

Above
The brass plaque dedicating the church organ to the memory of Frederick Colman.

Below
The console of the 25 aluminium pipe organ donated generously by Mrs. Helen Colman and her two sons Nigel and Gordon in 1915.

GREATER LOVE HATH NO MAN THAN THIS THAT A MAN LAY DOWN HIS LIFE FOR HIS FRIENDS

1914   THIS HAVE I DONE FOR THEE   1918

JOSEPH ARNOLD
FRED BILLING
WILLIAM BLAKER
ALBERT BOWLER
LEONARD BOWLER
VICTOR BOWN
ERNEST BRYAN
ARTHUR CULVER
MAURICE FURZE
FREDERICK GILES
WILLIAM GUDGEON
EDWARD LAWRENCE
W. LAWRENCE MANSFIELD

BERNARD MARSHALL
ERNEST MINNAY
FRANK C. MITCHELL
GEORGE H. MITCHELL
HORACE W. MITCHELL
ALBERT NASH
HERBERT J. PAGE
BRIAN DOLPHIN PAUL
ALFRED W. REED
SYDNEY F. RICHES
THOMAS H. RICHES
H.E. JOHN WALKER

GORDON BAKER
DAVIS BROWN
WILLIAM BUTLER
ALBERT CARPENTER
JOHN CLARK
STANLEY CULL
FREDERICK CUTTS
REGINALD DIXON
ERIC McMILLAN

STANLEY MAREWICK
WILLIAM NICHOLAS
HAROLD PEARSON
THEOPHILUS PYE
WILLIAM SELBY
ALFRED SMITH
PETER TUPPEN
HARRY VOSS
LESLIE YATES

1939   1945

watch them, and some to join with them and the girls of St. Monica's school in the service. On such occasions, even in my day, the church was practically full and the behaviour of the soldiers was all that could be desired.

I wonder whether Mr. Warwick remembers how on one Palm Sunday they listened so intently to his reading of the second Lesson, part of the Story of the Passion, that we remarked afterwards that the dropping of a pin could have been heard. They even listened to my sermons, and I loved talking to them, though I don't know what the girls of St. Monica's School thought of some of the things I said.

The battalion used to send occasional drafts over to France, and on those occasions I went over to Tattenham Corner, where the men were assembled, had a short service with them, and said a few words to the men who knew something of the horror they would be called upon to face. I undertook all this, as their chaplain was Vicar of a London parish and could only visit them on rare occasions.

I had been in the Parish twelve years when Duncan Woodroffe, who had been my Vicar all the time, died suddenly in the middle of a service in the Parish Church. This was in the autumn of 1917, and his death meant to me not only the loss of one of the best of friends, but also my departure from the Parish, for the Bishop of Winchester sent me to Rowledge Vicarage and appointed the Reverend A. W. Hopkinson to the Parish of Banstead."

Opposite
The side panel of the organ on which the names of those who were killed in the First and Second World Wars are listed.

Below
A Battalion of soldiers waiting to board the train at Tattenham Corner.

Above
Tadworth, the City of
London Royal Fusilier
Camp during the Great
War.

AFTER THE GREAT WAR

With the arrival in 1918 of the Reverend A. W. Hopkinson at All Saints, Banstead to replace the deceased Duncan Woodroffe and the departure of Harold Godefroy in 1917, St. Mary's had a new Vicar and in 1919 a new Curate - George Cole.

The Reverend Arthur Hopkinson seemed not to be very fond of St. Mary's. In his book, "A Pastor's Progress" he wrote:

"There was a much larger church at the Burgh Heath end of the parish, built to meet the needs of a growing district which failed to grow; so that the church was never full, and the work always seemed to languish."

He continued:

"It would have been much easier during my time if Burgh Heath had not been included in Banstead, for there were all the difficulties inseparable from a district church – divided authority, divided loyalties. There was no obvious boundary line between the two districts, one church was too small and the other too large. There was one Church Council for the two places, and Burgh Heath was dependent financially on Banstead.

On the other hand there were two lots of organisations to run, choirs, Sunday-schools, mothers' meetings, and so on. If I left the curate in charge of Burgh Heath to himself, I was blamed for neglecting part of the parish, while if I gave more attention to it, I was accused of interfering. I did my best, but failed to a great extent."

According to Elsie Dansey (nee Tree), she remembered that as a child, Arthur Hopkinson gave long intellectual sermons that seemed unintelligible to the children and possibly even to some adults as well!

Planning the War Memorial

As mentioned earlier, George Cole was the new Curate in charge of St. Mary's from 1919. One of his first tasks was to plan a suitable monument in the church to the men who came from Burgh Heath and who lost their lives in the Great War.

The residents of Burgh Heath, unlike those in Banstead, opted not for a stone War Memorial but for a Hall. Hence, the War Memorial Hall was built opposite the green. In addition to the hall, it was also decided to list the names of those who died in the war on the ash panels fitted to the side of the newly installed organ in the church.

Elsie Dansey remembers the Curate, George Cole, and her father, Mr. Tree, discussing the sign writing on the panel by the organ to commemorate the parishioners killed in the Great War. They both smoked cigarettes and blew clever smoke rings during their discussions!

More changes

In 1923, George Cole was replaced by Cyril Sheehan-Dare. According to Elsie, he played the organ during the service and occasionally, forgot to stop, and had to be reminded to continue the service!

Below
The top panel of the War Memorial in the church listing the names of those parishoners who were killed in the Great War. The sign writing was done by Mr. Tree.

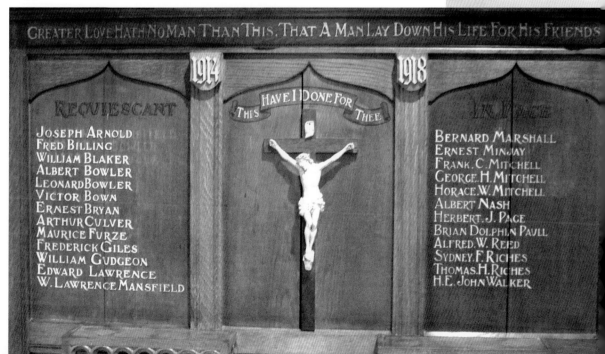

GREATER LOVE HATH NO MAN THAN THIS, THAT A MAN LAY DOWN HIS LIFE FOR HIS FRIENDS

1914   1918

REQUIESCANT

THIS HAVE I DONE FOR THEE

R.I.P.

JOSEPH ARNOLD
FRED BILLING
WILLIAM BLAKER
ALBERT BOWLER
LEONARD BOWLER
VICTOR BOWN
ERNEST BRYAN
ARTHUR CULVER
MAURICE FURZE
FREDERICK GILES
WILLIAM GUDGEON
EDWARD LAWRENCE
W. LAWRENCE MANSFIELD

BERNARD MARSHALL
ERNEST MINJAY
FRANK. C. MITCHELL
GEORGE. H. MITCHELL
HORACE. W. MITCHELL
ALBERT NASH
HERBERT. J. PAGE
BRIAN DOLPHIN PAULL
ALFRED. W. REED
SYDNEY. F. RICHES
THOMAS. H. RICHES
H.E. JOHN WALKER

In 1926, Cyril Sheehan-Dare was replaced by Frederick Kirby. The new curate was much loved by the children and held a children's service once a month instead of Sunday School.

In 1927, the Parish of Banstead was transferred to the new Diocese of Guildford.

SAINT MONICA'S CHAPEL

As mentioned earlier, the sittings in the church were free with the exception of the south chancel aisle, which was specially reserved for the accommodation of Mrs. Colman, her family, household and dependants as long as they remained in the parish. When the Nork Estate was sold for development in 1923 and Mrs. Colman and her family left the area the conditions of that appropriation lapsed. The south chancel could be converted into a chapel.

Due to the generosity of Miss Florence Bervon, Headmistress of St. Monica's School, a devoted supporter and sometime churchwarden of the church, a chapel to Saint Monica was built in the south chancel. There was no need for a Lady Chapel in the church since it was already dedicated to the Saint Mary the Virgin.

A faculty was raised on 2 August 1928 to convert the south chancel aisle into a side chapel by the erection of oak screens, an oak altar and other

Right
The Faculty issued on 2 August 1928 allowing the south chancel aisle in the church to be converted into a chapel.

By courtesy of Surrey History Centre

J O H N ————————— by Divine Permission BISHOP OF GUILDFORD To all Christian People to whom these Presents shall come or whom they shall or may in anywise concern and more especially to the Parishioners and Inhabitants of the Parish of BANSTEAD ————————— in the County of SURREY ————— and within Our Diocese and Jurisdiction. Greeting—Whereas a Petition has been presented to the Worshipful KENNETH READ MACMORRAN, Master of Arts, Bachelor of Laws, Our Vicar General and Official Principal of Our Consistorial and Episcopal Court of Guildford and filed in the Registry of Our said Court under the hands of The Reverend ARTHUR WELLS HOPKINSON Clerk Master of Arts Vicar of the Parish of BANSTEAD aforesaid and JOHN THOMAS REYNOLDS and GEORGE HARRY GREEN the Church-wardens of the said Parish

praying a Faculty to issue authorising the conversion of the South Chancel Aisle of the Church of Saint Mary the Virgin Burgh Heath in the said Parish into a Side Chapel by the erection of oak Screens and an oak Altar and other necessary fittings and furniture; also the placing of a Cross and Candlesticks in aluminium alloy on the said Altar and the insertion of stained glass in the East Window of the Chapel

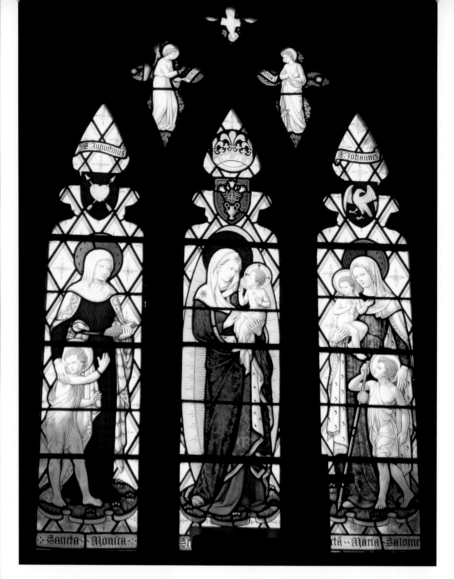

necessary fittings and furniture. Also the making and placing of a cross and candlesticks in aluminium alloy on the altar. A stained glass window was also to be inserted into the east window.

The work of the stained glass window together with all the fitments and fittings was undertaken by Sir John Ninian Comper (1864-1960) who was a remarkably flamboyant Anglo Catholic architect and designer who produced a vast body of work in both Anglican and Catholic churches throughout the world. His work was also much admired by John Betjeman.

Comper admired late-medieval glass for its "lightness and pearly whiteness" and has managed to achieve this in this beautiful window consisting of three uniform lights which depict Saint Monica and child Saint Augustine, Saint Mary the Virgin with child Jesus and Saint Mary Salome with child John.

CHAPTER 5
THE CHURCH BUILDING

The church was built between 1908 and 1909 by Messrs Roberts of Islington from the design by Mr. J. Alick Thomas. The building is in a restrained gothic style with the external walls of the church having a dressing of knapped flint. The the north and south sides of the church also have small buttresses along their length.

The parapets have a distinctive chequer-board pattern in alternating flint and stone squares. The small clerestory windows are set in sand coloured stone in a background of knapped flint.

The roof of red tile is at two levels, the chancel roof being a little lower. It is finished with decorative ridge tiles. Each of the three gables, one at each end of the roof and over the chancel arch, carries a stone cross. The aisle roofs are slated behind parapets which run the length of the building. The mullioned windows are in a decorated style.

THE ENTRANCES TO THE CHURCH

There are substantial double oak doors at the North West and the South West entrances. The South West entrance is the main entrance and the porch. The

Opposite
The West end of the church (2008)

Below
The church building viewed from the south. Notice the distinctive chequerboard pattern in alternating flint and stone.

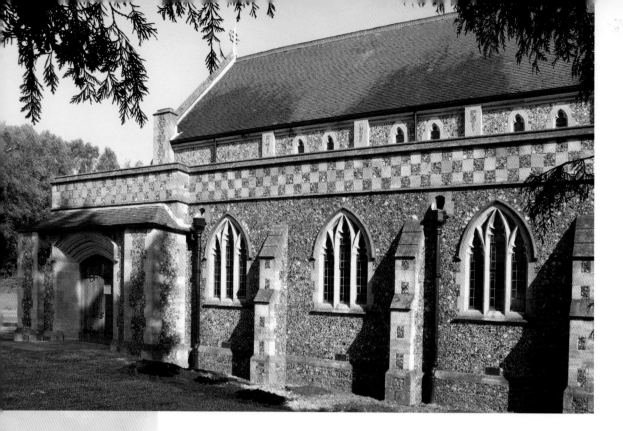

Above

The south west entrance
and the external wall of
the south aisle of the
church.

Notice the small buttresses
along the side and the
parapits which have a
distinctive chequer-board
pattern in alternating flint
and stone squares.

doors have substantial wrought iron hinges and hoop handles. They are bordered by stone with a decorative fluted hood mould above.

The North West entrance has a smaller porch, now replaced by a lobby serving the new accessible toilet. At the South East there is a personnel door which gives access to St. Monica's Chapel.

The Vestry is situated at the North East corner of the church. It has 2 large oak doors and there is also a small door to the Sanctuary from the priest's vestry.

THE EXTERIOR OF THE CHURCH OVER THE YEARS

The exterior of the church has changed little since it was built. The main changes have been in the surroundings. Originally, there was little or no vegetation growing. In time, a hedge was laid in front of the church and trees were planted. The main road was also further away from the front of the church.

In the past 30 years there has been a dramatic change to the surroundings. The main A217 road has been widened bringing the church closer to the road and the traffic. The front hedging has also been lost and the land surrounding the church has been resurfaced to accommodate a much needed car park.

Left
The church as it appeared
in the 1930s

*By courtesy of the
Banstead History Centre*

THE CHURCH BELL

A single bell is suspended in its own tower at the North East end of the
church close to the vestry.

Left
The single church bell
tower. (2008).

THE CHURCH INTERIOR

The ceiling of the Nave and Chancel is made of panelled timber boarding in the barrel style, which is a curved ceiling formed like a continuous arch. There are 6 corbels at each side of the church supporting the roof timbers..

THE SIDE AISLE CEILINGS

These are made of flat timber panelling which is angled at 22½ degrees to the horizontal.

PILLARS

There are 4 pillars on the north aisle and 3 on the south aisle. All are of uniform style but with 2 extra narrow sides to form gothic arches.

WALLS

The wall are generally painted plaster with facing stonework to the lower part of the Sanctuary walls.

WINDOWS

The windows are uniform in style. They are late Victorian Gothic in style. Each is mullioned and divided into small leaded panes.

NAVE

There are 4 triple lights in each aisle. One double light in the South West corner porch, one double light in the North West lobby and three slit windows are present at the west end set in a stone blind arcade.

Opposite
The panelled timber boarded ceiling of the Nave and Chancel.

Left
The flat timber panelled ceiling of the South aisle.

Overleaf
The Nave of the church looking towards the East window and Chancel

Clerestory

There are four pairs of small lights on each side of the nave

Chancel

The main East window consists of tall triple lights. There are two doubles on the North side and one double on the South side on the upper level.

St. Monica's Chapel

The windows are uniform in style. The main window is late Victorian Gothic triple lights, mullioned and the only stained glass in St. Mary's Church. The stained glass window depicts, from left to right: St. Monica and child (St. Augustine), St. Mary, Virgin with child Jesus and St. Mary Salome and child John the Baptist. Also on the south side there are 3 slit windows.

Memorials

There are three small memorials on the north wall of the Chancel. They are dedicated to Dora Beckett, Frederick Colman and Pat and Norman Kelly. A memorial to Bryan Dolphin Paull is fixed close to the south west door.

Above
The Chancel with the stone pulpit to the left of the picture.

Left
The organ donated by Mrs. Helen Colman and her sons in memory of Frederick Colman.

Overleaf
The Nave of the church looking towards the West window and font. The servery for dispensing refreshments before and after services is visible towards the right of the picture.

CHAPTER 6

YEARS OF GROWTH (1937 TO 1967)

At the start of 1937 St. Mary's was a daughter church of All Saints Banstead with Canon Frederick Skene as the Vicar and Francis Thornhill as the Curate in Charge of St. Mary's. As the congregation of St. Mary's had grown considerably over the years and due to administrative difficulties it was soon recognised that St. Mary's should be a parish in its own right. On July 6th 1937 the Parish of Burgh Heath was officially constituted with St. Mary's becoming the parish church and having its own Vicar and Parochial Church Council.

THE BOUNDARIES OF THE PARISH OF BURGH HEATH

The Parish of Burgh Heath at the time was about 2 miles from north to south, and about 2¼ miles from east to west. It was bounded by Kingswood Station, Waterhouse Lane, Shelvers Way, Epsom Lane, Yewtree Bottom Road, Reigate Road, The Drive, Garratt's Lane, Shrubland Road, Chipstead Road, Perrott's Farm and the railway to Kingswood Station. In all, there were thirteen miles of road, with 1,400 houses and about 4,500 people. The Church was also in the very centre of the parish with most houses within a mile of it. The Vicarage, however, was in one corner of the parish and about three quarters of a mile from the Church.

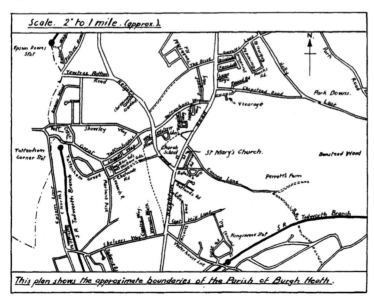

Opposite
The Reverend Arthur Leyland Bird with his wife Dolcie. (1950s)

Left
The boundaries of the Parish of Burgh Heath in 1938.

Above
The old Vicarage off
Chipstead Road.

Years later, it was sold by
auction on Tuesday
October 12 1965 to pay for
the new vicarage close to
St. Mark's Church.

THE APPOINTMENT OF THE FIRST VICAR

The new vicar for St. Mary's, appointed by the Bishop of Guildford, was
the Reverend Arthur Leyland Bird. He was educated at Marlborough
College and served as Curate of Holy Trinity, Middlesbrough from 1925 to
1931. He then served until 1937 as a Priest Brother of the Brotherhood of
the Good Shepherd Dubbs in New South Wales, Australia, and Rector of
Christ Church, Brewarrin, in the Bathurst Diocese. This comprised an area
of about 20,000 square miles, producing the finest Merino wool. During
1937 he served as an assistant priest at St. Thomas-on-the-Bourne,
Farnham. In his first letter in the Burgh Heath Parish magazine he wrote:

> *"I heard all sorts of terrible things about Burgh Heath before I came*
> *here, as I expect you did about me, and it is good to find that you are*
> *not as black as you were painted and I hope you are finding the same*
> *about your new Vicar!"*

According to recollections by Michael Woodman:

> *"..the Vicar was known affectionately as 'Dickie' Bird. During the time*
> *that he had spent in the Australian Bush "Dickie" met up with a*
> *striking lady who became his wife, Dolcie, after which they came to*
> *England and Burgh Heath. They had two children, a boy and a girl.*
> *They were a great family and much liked within the Parish of Burgh*
> *Heath and Great Tattenhams. Mrs. Dolcie Bird had a penetrating voice*

that could be heard after most church services. She was good for a laugh and could see the funny side of most things."

The new vicar had much to do. In addition to the usual clerical duties of running church services, there were PCC meetings to attend, groups and organisations to meet and encourage and the new parish magazine to edit and print. The Vicarage also had to be completed and furnished.

WAR BREAKS OUT

No sooner had the new Vicar settled down in the Parish than war broke out in 1939 and he was called up on September 4th and ordered to report that day for duty as an Army Chaplain. While he was away, Dudley Dixon was given charge of St. Mary's. Church services were held in daylight with no service being longer than an hour.

During his time as Army Chaplain, the vicar would write back home to his parishioners letting them know that he had not forgotten them. In a letter to the Parish Magazine in November 1939 he wrote from France:

"It seems years since I left Burgh Heath, but I haven't forgotten the place and the people. Please tell them that they are always in my prayers and give them my love and good wishes."

The Vicar went on to describe the confirmation, by the Bishop of Fulham, of seventy men and officers. The ceremony took place in a cinema to the musical accompaniment of six men playing mouth organs.

Finally in September 1943, the Vicar returned having been away for over 4 years. Needless to say he was glad to be back in his parish. Conscious of the fact that many parishioners were in the armed services, a Church Roll of Honour was created. By December 1943 the names of seventy-eight men and four women were on the Roll of Honour, three of whom had paid the supreme sacrifice. The Vicar made a point of praying for all those on the roll by name every Wednesday at 10 a.m. and once a month at Evensong on Sunday.

LOOKING TO THE FUTURE

Even as early as 1943, the vicar could see that the parish would grow considerably after the war and that there would be a need for another place of worship in the parish. In July 1945, at a meeting of the Parochial Church Council, the vicar reported that St. Mary's ranked high on the list for the provision of a Church Hall, a Church at Tattenham Corner and a stipend for a curate.

On the memorial, partially visible:

...LAWRENCE MANSFIELD

...ON BAKER
...S BROWN
...LIAM BUTLER
...ERT CARPENTER
...N CLARK
...NLEY CULL
...EDERICK CUTTS
...GINALD DIXON
...IC McMILLAN

STANLEY MARKW...
WILLIAM NICHOL...
HAROLD PEARSON
THEOPHILUS PYE
WILLIAM SELBY
ALFRED SMITH
PETER TUPPEN
HARRY VOSS
LESLIE YATES

Above
The War Memorial and the Book of Remembrance containing the names of all the local Parishioners who were in the services during World War II.

THE RE-DEDICATION OF THE WAR MEMORIAL

In March 1948, the Church Council decided that a memorial to those who gave their lives in the 1939-45 war would be placed in St. Mary's Church.

On Sunday evening, 6th November 1948, a large congregation gathered for the unveiling and dedication of the War Memorial. The Urban District Council, British Legion, Scouts, Guides, and the Methodist Church were all represented. The relatives of the fallen had special invitations.

While all stood in reverent silence, Brigadier Scott-Barrett unveiled the Memorial to those who had not returned and to those who came back from the deadly conflict of 1939-1945. None could have been unmoved as Canon Clitherow dedicated it, and quoted the immortal words "They shall not grow old..." from Laurence Binyon's poem. Many of those present must also have had memories of the shared dangers and hardships and of their comrades whose supreme sacrifice was honoured.

The Memorial consists of the addition of the names of the fallen to those already on the panels for the 1914-1918 War, a Book of Remembrance of those who served, in a beautiful carved oak case on a stand, and oak candlesticks and shelves for flowers. The lettering on the panels and the oak carving is the work of two members of the congregation.

In addition to the Memorial, a lovely set of Communion Vessels, dedicated by the Vicar on the Sunday morning, were made for the Church and had the following inscription on the chalice:

"To the Glory of God and in Thoughtful Remembrance of the Men of the Parish of Burgh Heath who gave their lives in the World War, 1939-1945. Requiescant in pace"

and on the ciborium:

"The Church of S. Mary the Virgin, Burgh Heath. 6th November, 1949."

ST. MARK'S CHURCH HALL

After years of planning St. Mark's Church Hall was built. The opening and dedication took place on the 6th October 1951. A congregation of nearly five hundred attended the historic occasion many of whom had to stand.

During the service the Lord Bishop of Guildford dedicated the font, lectern, prayer desk and altar and in his address said that just as Jacob's dream was the start of the great Temple at Jerusalem so they had to make St. Mark's, the House of God and the gate of heaven to the people living round it. Before the close of the service the Bishop gave a personal blessing to the three—Deaconess, Lay Reader and Vicar—who were charged with the spiritual oversight of the Church and district. After the service the assembled company was entertained to tea and inspected the building

A year later it was reported in the parish magazine for November 1952 that not only had the number of worshippers not grown in number at St. Mark's but they had actually fallen since the church was opened.

AN ASSISTANT CURATE FOR THE PARISH

It had been clear for many years after the war that the parish was in need of an assistant curate to help the vicar. In 1952, Brigadier Hugh Scott-Barrett a man, well known and held in great regard having served St. Mary's Church for many years, put himself forward as an assistant curate. This entailed going to St. Deiniol's Library, Hawarden, Chester for six months of theological training.

On Sunday 21st December 1952 at 10.30 a.m. Mr. Scott-Barrett, and Mr. Cutts, from Godalming, were ordained as priests by the Lord Bishop of Guildford in St. Mary's Church. This was a noteworthy occasion in the history of St. Mary's Church as ordinations are usually held in the diocesan cathedral.

IN LOVING REMEMBRANCE OF HUGH SCOTT-BARRETT, CB, CBE, ASSISTANT PRIEST OF THIS PARISH 1952 - 1958

Sadly, Reverend Hugh Scott-Barrett passed away in 1958. The carving of the last supper is dedicated to his memory and hangs behind the main altar.

THE END OF AN ERA

In the early part of 1956 the Vicar was taken seriously ill and did not fully recover until the middle of 1957. During that time the parish was looked after by the Reverend Hugh Scott-Barrett and the Reverend Roy Trevivian.

In January 1962, the Parish Magazine reported that the Vicar felt something was lacking at the Yuletide Fayre. Perhaps he felt that it was time for a change having spent nearly 25 years at St. Mary's. Later, in April, the Vicar announced that he would be leaving St. Mary's and that his successor would be the Reverend Peter H. Geake, Chaplain of Canford School in Dorset who would take over in September.

The Vicar gave his last service at St. Mary's on June 3 1962 and then left to take on the post of Vicar of St. Peter's Church, Walton on the Hill.

CHAPTER 7

TURBULENT TIMES

In June 1962, the Reverend Arthur Leyland Bird left with much sadness after 25 years as Vicar of St. Mary's. He had been the first Vicar of St. Mary's shortly after it was constituted as a Parish. In his time he had seen many changes, in particular the building of St. Mark's Church Hall in Tattenham Way which was also used as a church. This was to have a profound effect on the viability of St. Mary's in the years to come.

AN ACT OF VANDALISM FOILED

With little if any warning, the new Vicar, the Reverend Peter Henry Geake, abandoned the printing of the Parish Magazine which up until that time was published for 11 months of the year. This was an ominous sign.

The Vicar sent a letter on the 11 December 1962 to the Archdeacon informing him of the decision by the Parochial Church Council to explore the possibility of building the new church of St. Mark's. In addition, the Vicar also proposed a scheme to raise money for building the new church by selling off the old Vicarage and demolishing St. Mary's Church.

In reply to the Vicar, the secretary to the Archdeacon promised to notify the Church Commissioners of the Vicar's intentions and exploration of obtaining the appropriate applications for planning permission. It was also mentioned that the Vicar was within his rights to do so since the church was legally vested in the incumbent as part of the freehold and not in the Church Commissioners. Regarding the possibility of demolishing St. Mary's, the Vicar was warned

> " to make sure that the Central Council for the Care of Churches will support the demolition proposal (as) they have the power to resist any proposals on the grounds of architectural or other interest, which might be awkward if they exercised these powers at a late stage."

Regarding the old Vicarage, the secretary informed the Vicar that the Vicarage was the concern of the Dilapidations Board and that its Secretary had no objection to applying for planning permission and putting up a specific proposal later.

In the early part of 1963, the Vicar applied for permission to develop the site of St. Mary's by having it demolished and, in its place, erecting a petrol

filling station and garage. Thankfully, permission was refused for such an act of vandalism. It appears that the pastoral needs of the loyal band of churchgoers at St. Mary's were being neglected.

THE SALE OF THE OLD VICARAGE

Although permission to demolish St. Mary's was refused the Reverend Peter Geake continued with the second part of the plan which was to sell the old Vicarage and use the money to pay for a new Vicarage closer to what would become the new church of St. Mark's.

In May 1963, the Vicar, writing to the Diocesan Dilapidations Board, stated that:

> "It has been clear to me from the time I arrived in this parish that before very long it would be necessary to move the Vicarage. The existing Vicarage is a very pleasant house, but it is right in one corner of the parish."

He then put forward two alternatives. One was to enlarge the existing curate's house, which adjoins St. Mark's Church Hall. The other was to try to acquire a suitable house in the neighbourhood. In either case, the Vicar was intent on selling the old Vicarage.

At a meeting of the Burgh Heath Parochial Church Council held on 16 November 1964 it was agreed that

"the old Vicarage be sold and that the proceeds of this sale be applied to buying St. Mark's House from the Diocesan Board of Finance and also to the enlarging of that house to make it the Vicarage."

In June 1963, the Vicar obtained approval, in principle, to sell the old Vicarage and to purchase from the Parochial Church Council the present Curate's house and to enlarge it into a suitable Vicarage.

And so it came to pass that the old Vicarage was sold and the monies used to extend the Curate's house near to St. Mark's. The church of St. Mark's also became the Parish Church and St. Mary's became the daughter church.

DECLARING ST. MARY'S REDUNDANT

At a meeting of the Parochial Church Council on the 18th of November 1975 in the presence of the Reverend W. Purcell, Archdeacon of Dorking, a resolution was carried by fourteen votes to five with one abstention to

"..recommend that the Diocesan Pastoral Committee should now be asked to prepare a pastoral scheme for a declaration of redundancy to be made in respect of St. Mary's Church."

It was also stated that it was to be placed on record that the PCC took:

"..this difficult decision after much thought and prayer, and with a due sense of the responsibility with which (they had) been entrusted as members of the Parochial Church Council."

The Archdeacon stated that in arriving at this decision that:

"the Parish would be better served by concentrating both the financial resources and the holding of services to one Church only."

Regarding the procedure for declaring St. Mary's redundant he replied:

"..that there was ample opportunity for the interested parties to state their case. The Pastoral Committee would ask interested parties for their views; draft proposals would be drawn up for the approval of the Bishop, and the matter referred to the Church Commissioners. They would refer the matter back to the interested parties for comments which would be borne in mind when drawing up proposals. These proposals would be published, and representations could be made within 28 days before the final measure would be passed. A gap of one year would have to elapse before a decision on the use of the land could

be taken at the present time, although it was hoped that this period would soon be reduced. During this time, the responsibility for the building would pass from the PCC to the Diocesan Board of Finance."

In reply to a question on the reasons for the Pastoral Committee's decision, the Archdeacon stated that finance must be considered but the main concern of the Committee was pastoral considerations, and in their view these could best be served by having one church.

Mr. Rogers stated that logically St. Mary's should close, however money was not the only consideration, and people could be expected to fight the decision. Since St. Mark's was built, all efforts had been directed to paying off the debt and he had requested that St. Mary's be made a special project.

A question was also raised to confirm that the situation was to have two churches and one priest or one church and two priests, to which the Chairman replied that the stated choices were the true options. He also expressed sympathy to those, who for so many years, had worshipped at St. Mary's, but at the time when so many Christian organisations were so short of money, he questioned whether it was feasible to spend large sums on restoring a second church. He also concluded that the decision to pay off the debt on St. Mark's was undoubtedly the correct one in view of the current economic climate.

So a pastoral scheme was prepared for a declaration of redundancy to be made in respect of St. Mary's Church.

THE FIGHT FOR ST. MARY'S

A group of loyal worshippers at St. Mary's decided to oppose the misnamed pastoral scheme since it meant that St. Mary's would be declared redundant and so deprive them of a church that was built by the sacrifice, donations and gifts of the many people who lived in the area. Undaunted by the challenges ahead they decided to oppose the scheme vigorously.

On the 8th of December 1977 the proposals for redundancy were submitted by the Bishop of Guildford to the Church Commissioners. Representations were made against these proposals by the congregation of St. Mary's but were rejected by the Church Commissioners.

The proposals were then submitted to Her Majesty in Council for confirmation. A petition was also submitted by congregation of St. Mary's for an appeal to be heard by the Judicial Committee of the Privy Council. This was heard by Lord Edmund-Davies, Lord Scarman and Lord Lane on 17 November 1979.

THE JUDGEMENT

The judgement of The Lords of the Judicial Committee of The Privy Council on the closure of St. Mary's was delivered on 11th February 1980. Mr. R. E. Rogers and others were the Appellants and the Church Commissioners were the Respondents. Those present at the hearing were: Lord Edmund-Davies, Lord Scarman and Lord Lane. The judgement was delivered by Lord Lane.

Lord Lane stated that:

"The task which faces their Lordships in exercising the appellate jurisdiction under section 8 of the Pastoral Measure 1968 is unenviable."

He continued:

"There has been nothing in the nature of a judicial hearing or determination from which the appeal is made. Sections 3 to 7 of the Measure set out the steps which must be taken by the Pastoral Committee, the bishop and the Church Commissioners before any scheme for altering the arrangements for pastoral care and supervision in the diocese is submitted for confirmation by Her Majesty in Council. It is essentially an administrative decision which is the subject of appeal."

Lord Lane did point out however, that section 8(4) of the Measure provides that:

"....Her Majesty in Council may order that the appeal be heard by the Judicial Committee of the Privy Council, and the Judicial Committee shall make a report thereon and may propose to Her Majesty in Council that the appeal should be allowed, or dismissed, or that the scheme should be returned to the Commissioners for reconsideration...."

Lord Lane then outlined the scheme dated 25th November 1977 which concerned the church of St. Mary the Virgin, Burgh Heath. The scheme, which was to be the subject of the appeal:

"proposed that the church (St. Mary's), being a chapel of ease in the parish of Tattenham Corner and Burgh Heath in the diocese of Guildford, should be declared redundant and that the area covered by that parish should be transferred as to one part to the parish of Banstead, as to a second part to the parish of St. Andrew, Kingswood, in the diocese of Southwark, and that the third section should remain in the parish as before but should look to the church of St. Mark's as the proper place of worship."

He then went on to describe how the extensive housing development in the area led to the need for another church roughly in the centre of the Tattenham Corner development and about half a mile away from St. Mary's as the crow flies. Work on the new church of St. Mark the Evangelist started in 1966 which was then made the new parish church, with St. Mary's becoming a chapel of ease.

Lord Lane pointed out that:

"It is perhaps worthwhile to note that the parish raised no less than £24,025 towards the building of St. Mark's. The proponents of the scheme say that a choice must now be made between the two churches. Both, it is said, cannot continue to exist. One must be made redundant, and that must clearly be St. Mary's.

He also mentioned that:

"The basis of those contentions, it is fair to say, is primarily financial."

In particular, he continued:

"The matter is put in this way in paragraph R of the respondents' Answers

'In supporting the view ... that St. Mary's should be declared redundant the Committee was motivated by considerations of mission and pastoral care and in particular for the need for missionary work amongst the new housing estates at Tattenham Corner and the need for the Vicar in his work to have the help of an assistant curate whose stipend might not be able to be found if a considerable part of the financial resources of the Parish had to be applied in the repair and maintenance of St. Mary's.'

He then mentioned that:

"The appellants' case was presented with admirable clarity and economy of words by one of their number, Mr. R. E. Rogers. They believe, rightly or wrongly, that for very many years there has been amongst some of those who matter an ill-concealed wish for the end of St. Mary's. The start was certainly inauspicious. In 1962 the then incumbent, after only three months in that office and with little if any warning, applied to the Local Planning Authority for permission to develop the site by demolishing the church and erecting a petrol filling station and garage in its place. Permission was refused, but even at this early stage, a lack of enthusiasm (to say the least) about the continued survival of St. Mary's was all too apparent. Nevertheless in 1969 the Guildford Diocesan Pastoral Committee decided that St. Mary's had

not become redundant despite the building of St. Mark's two years before.

St. Mary's has since then, and particularly from 1976, suffered from the blighting effect of threatened closure. For 12 months there was no curate - the Vicar was on his own. Services were of necessity fixed at awkward times, and inevitably congregations became smaller. There is however no doubt that there is an enthusiastic if small body of worshippers who would be seriously affected by any closure. Equally there is no doubt that if services were held regularly and at reasonable times they would draw good congregations. A not inconsiderable number of new houses have been built near St. Mary's, though not to compare with the number at Tattenham Corner.

It seems to their Lordships that if one were to pay regard to pastoral care alone both churches are undoubtedly required. What the respondents say is that the money for that course is not available. What Mr. Spencer Maurice described as a "stark choice" lies between churches and manpower. If both churches are retained there will not be enough money to provide a curate to assist the vicar; if St. Mary's is declared redundant that will release the funds to pay for such assistance. Either, he contends one church and two clergy or two churches served by one parish priest.

That contention requires close examination. It is clear that when the matter was considered by the Parochial Church Council in 1976, they were under the impression that repairs and renewals to St. Mary's were a matter of urgency and could be delayed no longer, that there would be a deficit in the parish accounts of some £1,000 by the end of the year, and that the situation was such that it would mean financial ruin if both churches were to be kept alive."

Lord Lane surmised that:

"Those impressions were not correct. Both the urgency and the cost of repairs had clearly, albeit innocently, been exaggerated. There is now available from various sources some £5,620 for any work which requires to be done.

So far as the expected deficit was concerned, when the final accounts appeared in March 1976, so far from being a loss of £1,000 there was a credit balance of £2,000.

Moreover at the time of the meeting of the Parochial Church Council on 18th November 1975 when the Council voted to recommend the declaration for redundancy, the united parish was still paying off the debt for the building of St. Mark's. Only six weeks later the whole of that remaining debt had been discharged. That possibility does not seem to have been foreseen at the meeting."

Lord Lane then summed up that:

"Their Lordships appreciate that the way ahead may not be easy, but judging from what they have heard and read, there is a powerful and generous body of well-wishers who will make it their business to see that a revitalised St. Mary's will not lack the funds necessary for existence. Their Lordships do not believe that the dilemma posed by Mr. Spencer Maurice in reality exists. There is a real need for both churches and the continued existence of both will not impose any insurmountable financial burden."

He finally concluded that:

"Their Lordships have been convinced by the appellants that the scheme is not one which ought to be implemented and accordingly propose to Her Majesty in Council that the appeal should be allowed."

St. Mary's was saved.

THE AFTERMATH

The success of the appeal was met with rejoicing in the congregation of St. Mary's. It was met however, with dismay and disappointment by the Church Commissioners, the Bishop of Guildford, the Burgh Heath PCC and the Vicar. They were also disappointed that the appeal was allowed on financial grounds as their scheme was solely to meet the pastoral needs of the parish.

It is interesting to note that the Vicar made only a passing reference to the outcome of the appeal in his sermon on the Sunday following the judgement. This was clearly the outcome no one wanted, with the exception of the congregation of St. Mary's.

On the 24th March 1980, the Church Commissioners gave their formal notice of withdrawal of the Scheme to the Secretary of the Burgh Heath PCC. Soon afterwards, at the Archdeacon's instigation and to fulfil legal obligations, a quinquennial inspection was carried out on St. Mary's Church to ensure that all necessary repairs that had been postponed were now made.

CHAPTER 8

CHURCH KNEELERS

The humble kneeler or hassock is much sought after especially when you need to kneel down. Painstakingly made and embroidered by hand it often is ignored. It takes hours of dedicated planning and effort to make a kneeler. The stitching is hard on the fingers as the strong hessian material has to be strong to resist the wear and tear of the many knees which it must support over a lifetime.

The original kneelers were donated to the church in 1909 by Mr. Charles Garton of Banstead Wood together with the gift of chairs. Between 1927 and 1937, some of the kneelers were replaced with covers mainly in dark red and black. By 1947 many of the original kneelers were clearly wearing out and so the Parochial Church Council authorised the purchase of material to make 50 kneelers. The work for this was mostly undertaken by Mr. Westwood who was also assisted by Mr. Arthur Summerfield. The kneelers were finished in a blue fabric. An additional 20 more kneelers were made by Mr. Westwood between 1950 and 1951 with another 20 some time later.

In 1987, to commemorate the 50th Anniversary of St. Mary's Burgh Heath being made a parish it was decided to re-cover the 100 kneelers in use. The project started with a small group of workers mostly from the congregation with some local friends and a few from as far as Somerset and Suffolk. Double-thread canvas was used to embroider the kneelers in five main colours to complement the colours of the church furnishings.

Some designs are traditional but many are original. In particular, the altar rail kneeler, made in 1989, was embroidered in tapestry wool. All the kneelers are lined with strong calico and finally backed with hessian.

Overleaf
A selection of the kneelers re-covered in 1987.

Also, a view of the Main Nave with the chairs donated by Charles Garton some of which have the hassocks or kneelers resting on them. (1990s)

By kind permission of David Hodges

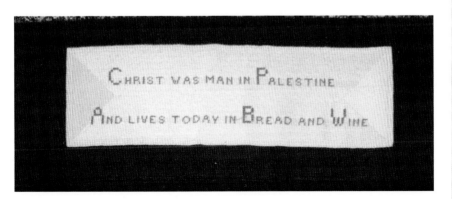

Left
The altar rail kneeler worked by Lillian Castle and bearing a quote by John Betjeman.

CHRIST WAS MAN IN PALESTINE
AND LIVES TODAY IN BREAD AND WINE

Regimental Cap Badge of 23rd Hussars
by Patricia Newman
in memory of Tpr. S.F. Cull

**Feather shapes in greens with
centre medallion**
by Mrs. H. Weller

Autumn Leaves
by Betty Stoessel

**Guildford Cathedral dedicated
to the Holy Ghost**
by Joan Grayson

"Jesus Christ the Apple Tree.."
by J.G and Elsie Dansey

Two White Crosses
by Lily Butler

Three Wise Men
by Peggy Greenfield

White Cross
by Mrs. H. Weller

Black Bird Flying
by Lucy Smith

Kneelers of St. Mary's Church

A selection of the kneelers that have been re-covered and beautifully worked in tapestry wool in a variety of colourful designs, many of them original

Hubert de Burgh
by Joy Henderson

Squares of Rhodes
by Mrs. H. Weller

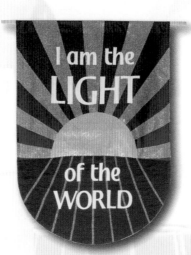

The set of six "I am" banners made by Christine Symes for the six spaces on the north and south walls.

CHAPTER 9
CHURCH BANNERS

Designing and making Christian banners is for me both a hobby and a ministry. In the past twenty-five years or so I have produced more than seventy banners, large and small. Some have been personal gifts for individuals, but the majority were intended for use in congregational worship. Most have been used locally; however a few were commissioned for other UK churches, and some hang in places of worship as far afield as Peru, Pakistan and the Philippines.

The banners are made from a variety of fabrics, mainly using a technique of appliqué with occasional embroidery, and a combination of hand and machine stitching. My banners are not intended merely as wall decorations – their purpose is to inspire, to encourage, to help in worship and above all to point to God. They take many hours to complete, and much prayer, as I can do nothing without the help of the Holy Spirit.

My husband Roger and I have loved being part of the church family at St Mary's since we came here from St Paul's in 2002. We are both retired, and are fully involved in the life of St Mary's, Roger on the buildings side among much else (having designed and overseen the various renovations that have taken place), and myself contributing to the music on keyboard and organ.

Soon after our arrival I made the set of six "I am" banners for the six spaces on the north and south walls, to give a fresh look to the building and convey a clear message about the Person of Jesus Christ. The Communion Table frontals with matching pulpit and lectern falls, the two small 'Mary' banners on the West wall and two Christmas banners followed.

Although recovering from a lengthy period of cancer treatment, I was glad to be invited to make a banner for St Mary's centenary. After much thought, prayer and work, the finished article (130cm x 190cm) has a relatively simple design. The shape of St Mary's is clearly depicted, but I wanted to convey the truth that the church essentially is people, not a building – people of all ages and types who meet under the cross of Christ. The bright colours of the figures indicate life and vibrancy, while the background colours are chosen to blend with the church furnishings. Though the relevant dates feature prominently, the statements at top and bottom emphasise that the story of St Mary's is ongoing, with much to look forward to.

Christine Symes

St Mary's Centenary Banner
made by Christine Symes

St. Mary's has often been under the charge of a curate as it only had its own vicar for a few years between 1937 and 1967 and has had less stability than most churches. In the past 100 years it has gone through several identity changes, from being a church plant in a school to having a building, from being in the parish of Banstead, to having its own parish, to becoming a daughter church of St Mark's Great Tattenham's, and now being a daughter church of St Paul Howell Hill within the parish of Howell Hill with Burgh Heath. It has also survived two threatened closures and now is again thriving. All of this has if anything strengthened the bond between the village community and the church community. It has also helped St Mary's to develop a strong lay leadership, to have an identity shaped by its members and to find its security in God rather than structures.

I was saddened to read about the threat to close St Mary's and very excited about the prospect of St Paul's being able to help. I discovered that I was living in the parish of Burgh Heath and in fact my house had been built on land from the old vicarage. I volunteered to get involved and although I was training for ordination in 2002, I helped out where I could, starting a toddler group very early on.

Below
The church in the early 1990s looking rather neglected with poor heating, dim lighting and uncomfortable chairs that left an impression on the sitter.

By kind permission of David Hodges

St Mary's took a lot of money to refurbish, many tens of thousands of pounds have been spent and without the sacrificial giving of the people of St Paul's and of St Mary's it would not have been possible. It is ironic that to build the church cost about £5000 but it has taken in the region of £170,000 to restore it and upgrade it both for comfort but also to provide adequate access and facilities for the disabled.

My early impressions of St Mary's were of a slightly neglected building, with poor heating and dim lighting and uncomfortable chairs but with a committed congregation who were eager to work with us to begin the process of refurbishment and revitalization. It has been a wonderful journey we have travelled together. Now St Mary's has a strong future ahead, there are once again young children involved in services with flags to wave and actions to show us, there is a mix of music with band and organ, there is modern technology and a working boiler, and better facilities. However every Sunday, as has been the case for 100 years now, people gather here who love God and who enjoy praising him, praying to him and learning about him.

Serving the community is still also at the heart of what St Mary's does and it has been great to have had the opportunity to open the Coffee Shop at 18 The Parade, Burgh Heath. This is an invaluable meeting place for people during the day, for children after school and for church meetings and the younger Sunday school group.

CHAPTER 11

HOW ST. PAUL'S AND ST. MARY'S GOT TOGETHER

The Bishop of Guildford in his visitation to the Epsom Deanery in 1999, reported:

"The Church is moving forward in good heart,"

as he enthused about the life and growth he saw in the parishes. However, in the same week the local press reported;

"Burgh Heath Church Closure Plan".

The story described a growing storm over diocesan proposals to close St. Mary's, as its congregation was tiny, elderly and unable to sustain the building, and its Parish Church, St. Mark's Tattenham Corner, did not have the resources to support it any longer. The faithful remnant of regular worshippers were devastated and the local population protested at the prospect of losing their landmark building and place of worship.

An impasse seemed inevitable.

HELP FROM AN UNEXPECTED SOURCE

The Vicar of St. Paul's Howell Hill, Rev. Steve Wilcockson, offered to help. He contacted the Rural Dean and suggested that, as St. Paul's had been eager to plant a church for some time, and had members in the Banstead and Burgh Heath areas, an all round solution could be found whereby St. Mary's was transferred to the care of St. Paul's and reinforcements and resources could be put in place to rescue St. Mary's.

St. Mark's would thus be relieved of its financial burden, the local community would keep their landmark building, the existing St. Mary's congregation could maintain their worship, the Diocese need not worry any longer about Burgh Heath, and God would not look like he was very publicly going out of business with the closure of an attractive building on a main road. Everyone would win!

Unfortunately, despite the support of the Rural Dean, the Diocese did not register any interest, and plans to make St. Mary's redundant continued to proceed. A year later, Steve Wilcockson had himself been appointed Rural Dean and used his position to argue for the plan he had put forward. There was a considerable amount of suspicion about this, but cautiously the Diocese agreed to allow exploration of the idea, while continuing to plan for the closure of the church. Things moved very slowly.

THE START OF A PARTNERSHIP

Eventually, a partnership began in September 2002, with about fifty St. Paul's people worshipping in a service separate from the Holy Communion Service attended by the original worshippers. The Vicar himself conducted worship at St. Mary's three weeks out of every four. New people joined and relationships between the two congregations grew until within a year it was mutually agreed to unite the services.

At last, in 2003, a formal transfer was completed, whereby St. Mary's and the surrounding area became part of the Parish of St. Paul Howell Hill. Problems over car parking were overcome thanks to the generosity of Aberdour School, allowing us the use of their school car park every Sunday and some midweek occasions. The lack of a Church Hall for children's work was met by hiring the War Memorial Hall each Sunday morning.

Next, work began restoring the church building – an initial project totalling about £70,000, including a major re-ordering and redecoration scheme which produced the light, warm, comfortable, attractive and welcoming atmosphere you will meet today as you enter St. Mary's.

As the weeks and months went by, many new people joined up with the church, attendances and offerings increased, children's ministry resumed, a close-knit community atmosphere developed, and work amongst teenagers was begun. Rev. Sandra Faccini was ordained Deacon in June 2004 and worked alongside the Vicar in developing the Burgh Heath ministry, and – on being made Priest after her first year in post – took over the major responsibility for the day to day running of St. Mary's.

Under Sandra's leadership, the church grew in strength and numbers, with new initiatives taking shape, including the Toddlers Group which began small but is now booming, and the Tea Club for senior citizens – a ministry they really appreciate. A Sunday Evening Service was begun. Involvement with local schools and ecumenical relationships with other churches in the area were developed.

THE NEED FOR FACILITIES

Right from the start, the Vicar could see that we would need our own facilities to provide an informal meeting place and a connection-point with the local community. He began to pray for one of the shops on the parade close to the church to become available. He particularly wanted the end shop nearest the church, if possible!

While he was away working in the USA in September 2005, he received

an email from Sandra saying, "The shop at the end of the parade is closing and will be available to let – what do we do?" He replied, "Get it whatever the cost!" Again, the people of St. Paul's and St. Mary's dug deep and found the £40,000 needed to restore the premises and the ongoing funds to subsidise a shop which is a facility for the community rather than a profit-making enterprise.

There followed several months of negotiations, planning permission, fund raising and then restoring the rather run-down premises. Finally, in September 2006, The Coffee Shop opened for business, and a church member, Jane Hawkins, joined the team as Shop Manager. Since then many people have been welcomed in for a haven of peace and refreshment, and many young people have found it a safe place as a drop-in after-school club. Two young workers connected with the Church – Dan Stevenson and Fran Jackson – have been employed to look after them and to run our Youth Congregation that now meets each Friday evening at the Coffee Shop.

COMPLETION

Before the restoration of the work at St. Mary's could be considered complete, two more important areas of work were urgently necessary.

First, we needed to instal a servery for the refreshments we serve before and after our Sunday services and at midweek meetings. This was completed in the Autumn of 2007, greatly improving the fellowship and

welcome we can offer to one another and new people as they join the church.

Second, we needed to re-landscape parts of our church grounds to give us better on-site car parking, and a proper disabled-access route to the main door of the church. This work was put in hand during 2008, rectifying the problems of mud and puddles that had beset the pathway to the church for many years.

GOD

So much has been done in such a short time – it can only be God who is behind all this! As we have prayed, doors have opened, people have come in, and resources of money and time have been freely given, in order to bring the original vision to reality.

THIS IS NOT THE END OF THE STORY

But we haven't quite finished yet!

Our next goal is to acquire a family home in which a full time minister based in the Burgh Heath Village itself can live and become part of the community. In this way, we hope to maintain our personal commitment to the people of Burgh Heath for many years to come, and to build up St. Mary's Church as a place where local people find a welcome, and can find the love of Jesus waiting for them.

As we approach the Centenary in January 2009, we believe that God has done a new thing for this part of our parish, and we want to give him all the glory and praise as we face a bright future together.